Bug Books
COCKROACH

Karen Hartley, Chris Macro
and Philip Taylor

www.heinemann.co.uk
Visit our website to find out more information about Heinemann Library books.

To order:
☎ Phone 44 (0) 1865 888066
🖷 Send a fax to 44 (0) 1865 314091
💻 Visit the Heinemann Bookshop at www.heinemann.co.uk to browse our catalogue and order online.

First published in Great Britain by Heinemann Library,
Halley Court, Jordan Hill, Oxford OX2 8EJ,
a division of Reed Educational and Professional Publishing Ltd.
Heinemann is a registered trademark of Reed Educational and Professional Publishing Ltd.

OXFORD MELBOURNE AUCKLAND
JOHANNESBURG BLANTYRE GABORONE
IBADAN PORTSMOUTH (NH) USA CHICAGO

Designed by Celia Floyd
Illustrated by Alan Fraser at Pennant Illustration
Originated by Ambassador Litho ltd
Printed by South China Printing in Hong Kong/China

ISBN 0 431 01822 7 (hardback)
05 04 03 02 01
10 9 8 7 6 5 4 3 2 1

ISBN 0 431 01827 8 (paperback)
05 04 03 02 01
10 9 8 7 6 5 4 3 2 1

British Library Cataloguing in Publication Data

Hartley, Karen
　　Cockroach. – (Bug books) (Take-off!)
　　1.Cockroaches – Juvenile literature
　　I.Title II.Macro, Chris, 1940 – III.Taylor, Philip, 1949 –
　　595.7'28

Acknowledgements
The publishers would like to thank the following for permission to reproduce photographs:
Ardea: P Goetgheluck pp6, 10, 22, E Lindgren p11, J Mason pp14, 24, 27, A Weaving pp12, 26;
Bruce Coleman Ltd: A Purcell p19, K Taylor pp13, 21, 23, 25, 28, C Varndell p16, R Williams p5;
Trevor Clifford: p29; NHPA: ANT p9, G Bernard p17, S Dalton p4, M Garwood p18, D Heuclin p20;
Okapia: M Kage p7, N Lange p8; Oxford Scientific Films: D Curl p15.

Cover photograph reproduced with permission of Bruce Coleman.

Our thanks to Sue Graves and Hilda Reed for their advice and expertise in the preparation of this book.

Every effort has been made to contact copyright holders of any material reproduced in this book. Any omissions will be rectified in subsequent printings if notice is given to the publishers.

Contents

Any words appearing in the text in bold,
like this, are explained in the Glossary.

What are cockroaches?

cockroach

Cockroaches carry harmful germs.

Cockroaches are insects that live in lots of different countries. They are **pests** because they carry harmful **germs** which can make people ill.

There were cockroaches in the world about 300 million years ago when dinosaurs were living.

There are more than 3500 different kinds of cockroach. Most of these live in the **tropics**.

Cockroaches similar to this one lived millions of years ago.

leaf

What do cockroaches look like?

legs

Cockroaches carry harmful germs.

flat body

Cockroaches have quite flat bodies with three main parts. They have six long, slim legs. Their bodies look as if they made of shiny plastic.

Cockroaches have two pairs of wings. They have a pair of long **feelers** on their heads. They have long, hairy legs and small claws on their feet.

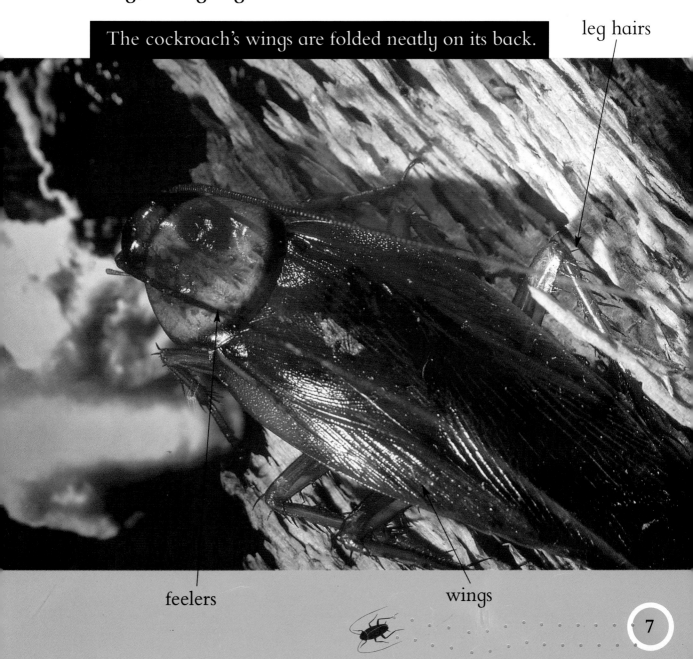

The cockroach's wings are folded neatly on its back.

leg hairs

feelers

wings

How big are cockroaches?

small cockroach

leaf

Some cockroaches are quite small.

Some cockroaches are big and some are small. In
Europe, the cockroaches are quite small and some
of them can fit on a small button or a 5p coin.

Draw round a small button to see
how little a cockroach can be.

8

Cockroaches in hot countries can be much bigger. Some can be 9 centimetres long! Look at the differences in the sizes of this cockroach and ant.

Some cockroaches are very big.

large cockroach

ant

Draw a 9 cm line on a piece of paper to see how big a cockroach can be.

How are cockroaches born?

Some **females** lay their eggs in cases. These cases are sometimes called purses. The purses protect the eggs and stop them from drying out.

The purse protects the developing eggs.

purse

Young cockroaches are called **nymphs**. As they get bigger, their skin cannot stretch, so they grow a new skin and **moult** the old one.

nymph

This young cockroach has just moulted.

old, empty skin

Baby cockroaches only grow wings when they hatch from their egg.

How do cockroaches grow?

Some cockroaches will carry their eggs until they are ready to hatch. This might take eight weeks.

nymphs

Baby cockroaches take up to eight weeks to hatch.

adult
cockroach

Some cockroaches **moult** and lose their old skin about once a week. They do this six or eight times before they are fully grown.

A cockroach will moult up to eight times before it is fully grown.

nymph

What do cockroaches eat?

centipede

cockroaches

These cockroaches are eating a dead centipede.

Cockroaches mainly eat dead plants and animals.
But they will eat almost anything.

Cockroaches will even eat the glue
from the back of postage stamps!

Some kinds of cockroaches live in hot countries like Barbados. They eat lots of different things there. They especially like the wood from dead trees.

This cockroach likes to eat wood from dead trees.

Which animals attack cockroaches?

Frogs eat cockroaches when they can catch them.

frog

Lizards, frogs and birds like to eat cockroaches if they can catch them. In places like India and South America, some people will catch cockroaches and eat them.

ants

Ants will sometimes attack cockroaches.

Other insects sometimes eat cockroaches. Some cockroaches can roll into a ball or tuck in their legs to protect themselves.

Where do cockroaches live?

A cockroach on a leaf.

leaf

Most cockroaches like to live in warm places and cannot **survive** in cold places. In Europe, many live in warm buildings, but there are some kinds that live outdoors in the grass and in bushes.

Cockroaches are **scavengers**. They like to live in bakeries, kitchens and restaurants where they can find food.

Health inspectors check restaurants and bakeries for cockroaches.

Most cockroaches like to live where there is plenty of food!

19

How do cockroaches move?

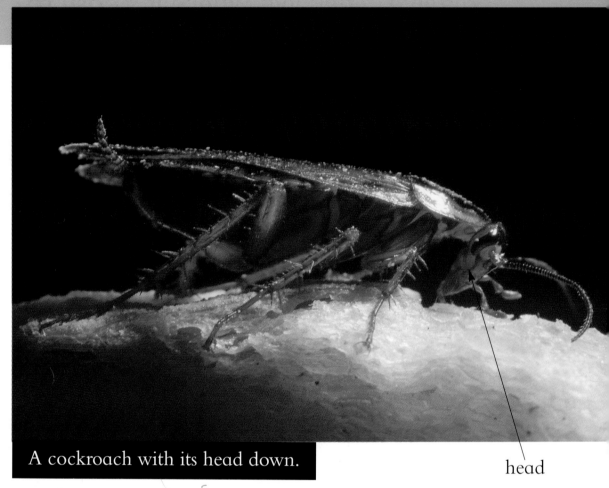

A cockroach with its head down.

head

Cockroaches have long legs and can run fast.
They usually move with their heads down so
that they can search the ground for food.

Some cockroaches in the **tropics** are the fastest
insects on land. Some can move at 5.4 km an hour.
That is 50 times their body length in a second!

wings

A female cockroach.

Even though they have two pairs of wings, only some cockroaches can fly. The females have smaller wings and very few of them can fly.

How old can cockroaches be?

A cockroach seen from below.

Some cockroaches live for a few months. Others can live for two or three years and can take one and a half years to become fully grown **adults**.

The temperature makes a difference to how long the adult cockroaches will live. They live longer when the weather is cool but not when it is too cold.

A cockroach lives longer in cool weather.

What do cockroaches do?

Cockroaches look for food at night.

Most cockroaches are **nocturnal** so they come out to look for food at night. Some kinds of cockroach will run away if they see a bright light.

food

Cockroaches are a danger to humans when they crawl over our food.

Cockroaches are called **pests** because they crawl over our food and leave dirt and **germs** on it.

People can get food poisoning if a cockroach crawls over their food.

25

How are cockroaches special?

Cockroaches are very important to both plants and animals because they make the soil better. They break up dead leaves and animal **droppings**.

Cockroaches break up dead leaves.

dead leaves

feelers ———————>

The feelers on a cockroach's body help it to sense danger.

Cockroaches have two special **feelers** on their bodies. These can feel the air being moved when other animals are close. This tells the cockroaches when they are in danger.

Thinking about cockroaches

See if you can answer these questions about cockroaches.

- Why does this **female** cockroach carry a special purse with her?

The female cockroach carries a special purse.

purse

- We move air to keep us cool. What does moving air tell a cockroach about other animals?

Bug map

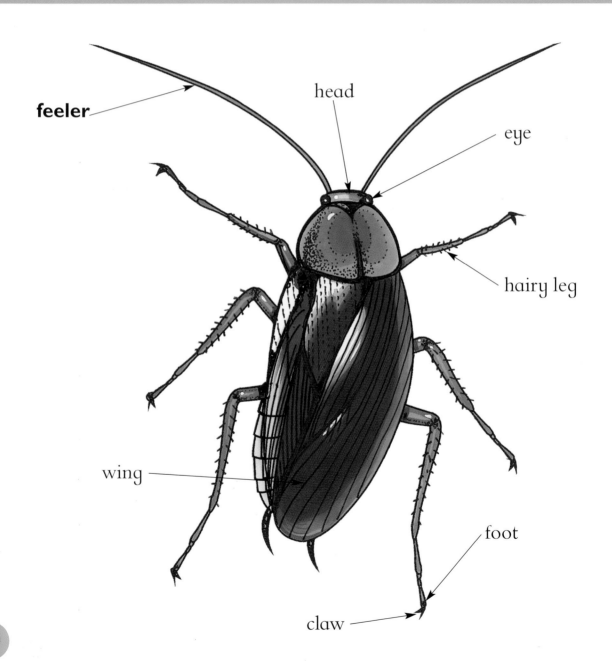

feeler

head

eye

hairy leg

wing

foot

claw

Glossary

adult	grown-up
droppings	body waste from an animal
feelers	thin growths from the head of an insect that help the insect to know what is around it
female	girl or mother animal
germs	tiny creatures that cause diseases
hatch	come out of its egg
insect	a small animal with six legs
moult	what happens when a young insect grows too big for its skin: it grows a new one and wriggles out of the old one
nocturnal	sleeps in the day and comes out at night
nymph	baby insect
pest	animal that is a nuisance to people
scavenger	animal that eats dead plants and other dead animals. Cockroaches also eat leftover scraps of food.
survive	able to live
tropics	the area of the Earth near the Equator, where it is warm the whole year round

a
b
c
d
e
f
g
h
i
j
k
l
m
n
o
p
q
r
s
t
u
v
w
x
y
z

31

Index

Titles in the *Bug Books* series include:

Hardback   0 431 01822 7

Hardback   0 431 01821 9

Hardback   0 431 01823 5

Hardback   0 431 01820 0

Find out about the other titles in this series on our website www.heinemann.co.uk/library